5-67

⤸ *H. L. Mencken*

BY PHILIP WAGNER

UNIVERSITY OF MINNESOTA PRESS • MINNEAPOLIS

Printed in the United States of America at the
Jones Press, Minneapolis

3 ☙❦☙ 2

Library of Congress Catalog Card Number: 66-64595

The author acknowledges permission to reprint passages from
the following works by H. L. Mencken: *Notes on Democracy*,
copyright 1926 by Alfred A. Knopf, Inc.; *Happy Days*, copyright 1940 by Alfred A. Knopf, Inc.; *Newspaper Days*, copyright 1941 by Alfred A. Knopf, Inc.; *A Vintage Mencken*, ©
copyright 1955 by Alfred A. Knopf; *Minority Report*, copyright 1956 by Alfred A. Knopf, Inc.; *Prejudices: A Selection*,
© copyright 1958 by Alfred A. Knopf, Inc.; *Letters of H. L.
Mencken*, © copyright 1961 by Alfred A. Knopf; *H. L.
Mencken on Music*, © copyright 1961 by Alfred A. Knopf.
He also wishes to acknowledge permission to use excerpts
from William Manchester's biography, *Disturber of the Peace*,
copyright 1950 by the author, on which he has also leaned for
names and chronological details.

PUBLISHED IN GREAT BRITAIN, INDIA, AND PAKISTAN BY THE OXFORD
UNIVERSITY PRESS, LONDON, BOMBAY, AND KARACHI, AND IN CANADA
BY THE COPP CLARK PUBLISHING CO. LIMITED, TORONTO

H. L. MENCKEN

PHILIP WAGNER, who succeeded H. L. Mencken as editor of the *Baltimore Evening Sun*, retired as editor of the *Sun* in 1964. He writes a syndicated newspaper column on public affairs and is the author of a number of books on wine growing.

⤹ *H. L. Mencken*

Henry Louis Mencken died in his sleep of a coronary occlusion on Sunday, January 29, 1956, in the row house on Hollins Street in Baltimore where he had lived most of his life. At midday on Tuesday a few people met at the neighborhood undertaker's just down the street: his brothers August and Charles and his sister Gertrude; Hamilton Owens, the chief editor of the Baltimore Sunpapers at that time; Alfred Knopf, his publisher; James Cain, the confectioner of hard-boiled fiction; the musician Louis Cheslock, most faithful of friends; and some others — fewer than a dozen in all. Hamilton Owens had been invited by August Mencken to preside. He rose, said briefly that they came together, as Henry had wanted, a few old friends to see him off, then sat down. The undertaker's men in their black suits took the body away, to the crematory, followed only by brothers August and Charlie. The company sat about uneasily for a few minutes and then scattered into the winter day.

The funeral of an unbeliever is more somber than most, since the usual remarks about a life everlasting are out of bounds. This one must have set some sort of record for bleakness, for in a way it was redundant. Mencken had been leading a ghostly life, "ready for the angels," since the day eight years before when he was knocked out by a cerebral thrombosis that affected his speech and partly paralyzed him. He recovered fully though slowly from the paralysis but was left cruelly handicapped in other ways, robbed of the ability to read and write, unable to remember the names even of his friends. Seen on one of his rare public appearances he appeared no different at first. He had been restored to what, following an earlier illness, he had called his "former loveliness": the dumpy figure that he liked to call matronly, the ruddy face, the scowl, the laugh, the popping blue eyes. But this was a deception. The croak of his voice was the same, but the words that issued were those of a stranger. The shell was intact, but the essence had been shattered; and the grim jest of it was that Mencken knew this deep inside as well as anyone else and yet was helpless to do anything about it.

But though he had to endure that long winter of wordlessness, it was surely not true that his career had been cut short. His daily newspaper work embraced better than half a century. The first and the last things he wrote for publication were printed in newspapers, and it must be remembered that Mencken thought of himself as a newspaperman before anything else. The flood of his critical writing, in the old *Smart Set* magazine mainly (the best of it republished in his *Prefaces* and *Prejudices*), swept away the deadening literary standards, and the deadly standard-bearers, of our early twentieth century and cleared the way for a tremendous flowering of new writing. As a slashing and wonderfully comic critic of American life and institutions he attained for a time a stature and influence such as no other American writer has ever known. Though he disclaimed scholarly pretensions, his *The American Language* systematically explored for the first time our native tongue as it must be distinguished from British English and provided a solid basis for American linguistics. As a political commentator he carried immense authority for a time — though this waned with the coming of that upheaval called the New Deal and was gone entirely by the time he had ceased writing. He wrote a formal treatise each on political theory, religion, and ethics. He tried his hand at verse and the drama. And the autobiographical sketches brought together in his *Days* books re-create the life of an American city, Baltimore, at the turn of the

6

century with such gusto and uproarious humor and unabashed sentiment that their claim to immortality is secure. All this — and his letters, too. Mencken the writer was cut down cruelly, but not cut short.

Mencken was third-generation Baltimore German. Baltimore was one of the chief ports of entry for the big German immigration of the mid-nineteenth century — the Forty-Eighters. Most of them moved on to make their main impression on the land and life of the Midwest. But many found Baltimore congenial, with its already well-established German community, and went no farther. Mencken's grandfather Burkhardt was one of these. Stiff-necked, immensely proud of the Mencken family's long roll of learned men, diligent and thrifty, he prospered in the tobacco business and founded a numerous family. His eldest son August held likewise to the tobacco business, prospered, and married Anna Abhau, daughter of another German Forty-Eighter.

It was into this conventional west Baltimore German family where values were certitudes, love and discipline were dispensed with a lavish and impartial hand, and security was never in question that Henry Louis Mencken was born on September 12, 1880. Insofar as any childhood can be easy, his was. "We were lucky," he wrote many years later of this childhood, "to have been born so soon," and he looked back at his childhood and indeed at the life it had prepared the way for without any regrets at all: "If I had my life to live over again I don't think I'd change it in any particular of the slightest consequence. I'd choose the same parents, the same birthplace, the same education (with may-be a few improvements here, chiefly in the direction of foreign languages), the same trade, the same jobs, the same income, the same politics, the same metaphysic, the same wife, the same friends, and (even though it may sound like a mere effort to shock humanity), the same relatives to the last known degree of consanguinity, including those in-law." It may not be far from the truth to say that he took the lonesome integrity of his mind and spirit from tough old Burkhardt, from his father August a talent for gaiety in company, and from his mother certain qualities that rarely show in his writing, especially his unexpected gentleness, his instant sympathy for the troubled, and his devotion to family life and routine.

His education moved ahead in the Baltimore German way, which is to say with the solidest kind of family backing. At the age of six he was handed over to Professor Friedrich Knapp and his thoroughly Teutonic Institute, a no-nonsense place, and did well in most subjects. In due course he was translated to a public high school, the Polytechnic Institute, where the main emphasis was then and still is on science and technology. This change was made by his father in the mistaken belief that little Harry had an aptitude for such matters. Though in his own words little Harry "had no more mechanical skill than a cow" he was tempted for a time by the mysteries of chemistry and photography and he was graduated — he was not quite sixteen — at the head of his class, even winning the competition for a gold medal in electricity. So much for science and his formal education.

His education in letters was a parallel and separate thing. The Mencken family was not particularly bookish, but there were books around, and the magazines of the time, and his introduction to the delights of the printed word came when he was seven by way of *Chatterbox*, the hard-cover annual which started generations of young English gentlemen on their way to literacy. He absorbed it so thoroughly, Englishness and all, that in middle life he confessed to knowing "more about Henry VIII and Lincoln Cathedral than I know about Millard Fillmore or the Mormon Temple at Salt Lake City." Young Henry dutifully did all the things the boys of his neighborhood were expected to do — he was a member in good standing of the neighborhood gang, he frequented the firehouse. But such occupations had to compete with "a new realm of being and a new and powerful enchantment" and before very many years had lost the battle. The "powerful suction of beautiful letters" had caught him and he never again escaped. He tackled Grimm's fairy tales — not much to his taste. He began to explore the contents of the old glass-front secretary that stands to this day in the Hollins Street middle sitting room with most of the same books still in it, a miscellany of things pretty much beyond his ken, hence all the more intriguing. And then he came upon *Huckleberry Finn*, "probably the most stupendous event of my whole life." The story of this encounter is set down in his sketch "Larval Stage of a Bookworm." By the age of nine he had his card for the neighborhood branch library and had begun "an almost daily harrying of the virgins at the delivery desk." He was caught for fair: "I began to inhabit a world that was two-thirds letterpress and only one-third trees, fields, streets and people. I acquired round shoulders, spindly shanks, and a despondent view of humanity. I read everything that I could find in English, taking in some of it but boggling most of it. . . . to this day [at 60] I am still what might be called a reader, and have a high regard for authors."

A second stupendous and decisive event is confessed in another of his sketches, "In the Footsteps of Gutenberg." It was the gift from his father, not long after his discovery of the magic of Mark Twain, of a toy printing press, a Dorman No. 10 Self-Inker costing $7.50 together with a font of No. 214 type costing $1.10. Mark Twain had made him a consumer of letters; this made him a producer. It put "the smell of printer's ink up my nose at the tender age of eight, and it has been swirling through my sinuses ever since." Other Christmas presents came along, to divert him mo-

9

mentarily — the set of water colors, the camera, the microscope, the galvanic battery, the set of carpenter's tools. But "it was the printing-press that left its marks, not only upon my hands, face and clothing, but also on my psyche. They are still there, though more than fifty years have come and gone."

His father, sensible man, saw Harry as logical heir to the tobacco business and had small patience with the notion of a career in writing or publishing. Henry was required to learn the rudiments of the business, including the way to roll a cigar. This was the cause of some friction between father and son, but there was never the slightest doubt in Henry's mind that the tobacco business was not for him, and, to cut the story short: "When, on my father's death, as I was eighteen, I was free at last to choose my trade in the world, I chose newspaper work without any hesitation whatever, and, save when the scent of a passing garbage-cart has revived my chemical libido, I have never regretted my choice. More than once I have slipped out of daily journalism to dally in its meretricious suburbs, but I have always returned repentant and relieved, like a blackamoor coming back in Autumn to a warm and sociable jail."

And so it was, four days after his father's death in 1899, that he presented himself at the office of one of Baltimore's several newspapers, the *Herald*, and was turned down. But his persistence earned him free-lance assignments, then a staff job. He soon demonstrated his ability and moved swiftly through every job in the office: police reporter, drama critic, Sunday editor, city editor, and by 1906 at the age of twenty-five actually the editor of the paper — only to see the *Herald* fail for reasons with which he had nothing to do, and to find himself out of a job.

It was then that he joined the *Sun* (locally the Sunpaper), a newspaper believed by the local gentry to be the one true source of wisdom and current intelligence, which remained his journalistic home to the end of his career. He did venture away from time to time for reasons that were various, but always returned "repentant and relieved." His connection with that paper (and its evening sister) turned into something unique in American journalism. The *Sun* provided the real launching pad for his career as a national figure and in turn gained immeasurably from the relationship.

From the beginning, however, he did not limit his writing to daily journalism, prodigious though his output for the *Herald* was. He began experimenting with verse, and selling it. He was a "stringer" providing features for out-of-town papers. He became a fabricator of short stories for most of the popular magazines of the day — formula fiction loaded with blood and thunder, done by the yard and showing small trace of the style we think of as Mencken's. He was available for hack jobs — even doing a prospectus for Loudon Park Cemetery, where, fittingly, his gravestone now stands. He didn't stop reading, either. He was sopping up the new writers who had things to say and said them well, such men as Shaw and Conrad; and always Mark Twain; and others such as Huxley and Nietzsche and Spencer and James Huneker and William Graham Sumner, the author of *Folkways*. They fixed his philosophical bearings once and for all (though these had been pretty well set already), and on them he honed his ideas and his style.

The hack period began to recede, and in 1905 he published his "first real book," as he called it, *George Bernard Shaw: His Plays* (he preferred not to count a little book of rather dreadful verse that too much fuss was later made about simply because copies were rare: the poetic muse kept clear of him always). This essay offered the first intimations of the Mencken style and his formidable critical capacity, immature though they were. It was no great success though it was well reviewed, but for him it broke the ice:

he was a published critic. Mencken recalled, in his *Newspaper Days*, his enchantment on the arrival of its proofs. His editor at that time, an understanding man named Meekins, insisted that he take the day off to read them. "So I locked myself in as he commanded, and had a shining day indeed, and I can still remember its unparalleled glow after all these years."

Three years later he published his *Philosophy of Friedrich Nietzsche*, a better book and still very much worth the reading. William Manchester, in *Disturber of the Peace*, best of the several Mencken biographies and studies, says, "The subject . . . was Mencken's Nietzsche, not Nietzsche's Nietzsche. There is a difference." It is probably a better guide to Mencken than to Nietzsche, to the extraordinary toughness and stiffness of his mind beneath its lively movement at the surface. He alluded to this quality himself from time to time. In a letter to the writer Jim Tully in 1940 he said: "I never listen to debates. They are dreadful things indeed. The plain truth is that I am not a fair man, and don't want to hear both sides. On all known subjects, ranging from aviation to xylophone-playing, I have fixed and invariable ideas. They have not changed since I was four or five years." And I remember a casual remark he made to me at about the time of that letter, when his thinking was going so strongly against the national grain. Speaking of another newspaper editor he said: "John is a reasonable man. Try it on him. A good argument will always fetch him, but not me." He was not boasting. Neither was he confessing. He was stating a fact.

There was another and important branching out early in his association with the *Sun*. Mencken's duties as an editorial writer were not arduous and they used up only a portion of his energy. A chance encounter with Theodore Dreiser, then a magazine editor, led him to another chance encounter with George Jean Nathan; and out of that all-day meeting of two men as unlike as two could be, yet so surprisingly alike in their disgust with contemporary life and letters, there came a partnership that lasted better than two decades. The inspiration of the partnership was a magazine of dubious reputation, the *Smart Set*, which was about to undergo one of its rejuvenations, or reincarnations. Mencken had been invited to do a monthly full-length piece for it on books, Nathan to do dramatic criticism. The result was something like a volcanic eruption. The shallow standards and appalling inanity of most American writing and the theater of the early years of this century were the targets of both. With high spirits, total confidence in their own judgments, and a torrent of brilliant invective, they laid about them, bashing heads, pulling down idols, puncturing inflated pomposity, infuriating the sources of conventional wisdom, sweeping away the rubbish that then passed for literature and drama. Prodigious labor was required, and it was a bravura performance. Mencken's stint was a monthly article of about five thousand words, and his anthologist Huntington Cairns, adding it all up, found that from November 1908 to the end of December 1923 he performed it one hundred and eighty-two successive months for a total of better than 900,000 words. The preparatory reading involved in this may be imagined. Mencken was equal to it because he was one of those reading prodigies who can gulp down books a page at a time missing nothing of consequence.

As contributors the two dominated the magazine, which was by no means an appropriate medium for such intellectual high jinks but better than none. In due time (1914) the magazine became theirs as joint editors. As editors they wrote much of it themselves under a fragrant bouquet of pseudonyms. Betty Adler, the Mencken bibliographer, has tracked down and confirmed 23 pseudonyms and lists 13 more as probabilities; the chances are there were others, used interchangeably or jointly by the two.

But they also searched out new talent, so buttressing their criticism with evidence of what they did like. Sweeping out the rubbish was not enough. They wanted non-rubbish to replace it, and this they set about discovering — a labor at which Mencken proved remarkably adept. Once he got on the scent of a promising writer he was unshakable — he cajoled, browbeat, sent gifts, fed ideas. There is a large risk of error in this hunting out of new writers, but he was equally skillful at ditching whatever failed to make the grade.

The *Smart Set* was a tour de force, a gale of fresh air across the campuses, a serial spoof, bellwether of a new generation, an object of delighted devotion.

Mencken and Nathan worked out a modus for editing which reduced red tape to zero. Nathan held down the New York office with the help of a secretary of monumental impassivity, a Miss Golde. Mencken did his reading, writing, and scouting for talent, and carried on his enormous correspondence, from his quarters on the third floor of the family home in Hollins Street, periodically taking the train to New York for a day which he and Nathan divided between merrymaking and the planning of the next issue.

But I get ahead of the story. Not long after Mencken's emergence through the *Smart Set* as a national critic of letters, things began to happen to the *Sun* in Baltimore. The *Sun* of that day was a staid institution much impressed with its rectitude and infallibility, one of the four pillars of Baltimore life, along with the Washington Monument, the Shot Tower, and Federal Hill, and just about as exciting. A victim of complacency and accumulated inhibitions, it began to go down hill even as a commercial enterprise, and it was sold to a group of wealthy Baltimore citizens headed by an aggressive publisher, formerly a competitor, who was resolved to pump some life back into it. The decision was made to spawn an evening sister, and to Mencken fell the task of providing this new *Evening Sun* with a personality and point of view, mainly by way of its editorial page. This he set about doing; and so (1911) his column, "The Free Lance," came into being. He was given a free hand, and took every advantage of this and of the title. The column swiftly became the sort of thing that no one of consequence in Baltimore dared not to read; and the subjects were whatever came into his head. Baltimore had seen nothing like it before. He was into everything: the mucky world of municipal politics, local forms of beastliness and gentility particularly when combined in the same person, new trends in writing, the deplorable condition of the sewage and water systems as reflected in the local typhoid death rate, the barbarous condition of the national culture — everything. The predominant qualities Mencken endowed the *Evening Sun* with were impertinence, riotous good humor, a high degree of literacy — with the back of the hand for every form of sham and a strenuously libertarian bias.

Mencken's output, not confined to the column by any means, was large. But thanks to the compulsive orderliness of his mind he worked with extraordinary economy. Pieces done for the *Smart Set* were reworked for the "Free Lance" column; "Free Lance" material found its way rearranged and expanded into the magazine; and much of all this eventually wound up in his books: the *Prejudices, The American Language, Notes on Democracy,* and so on. Mencken was never the man to waste a good thing on a single audience.

So things went for Mencken in the years before World War I, exuberantly, as he juggled two careers: those of a literary critic of rapidly growing stature and of a newspaper columnist knowing no bounds except those of libel and common prudence. There was no time for larger works, though these had begun to gestate in his mind; and the only thing that appeared between hard

covers was his priceless little drama without words, *The Artist,
a Drama without Words* (1915), which was later reprinted in his
A Book of Burlesques (1916).

But as the war approached, he found himself under growing
constraint in both careers. He was, to put the matter shortly, pro-
German. As he explained his position toward the end of the war
to a correspondent, the medical historian Fielding Garrison, "The
fact is that my 'loyalty' to Germany, as a state or a nation, is absolutely nil. I haven't a single living relative there; I haven't even a
friend there. . . . But I believe I was right when I argued that
unfairness to [the Germans] was discreditable and dangerous to
this country, and I am glad I did it." Other things — pride of an-
cestry, his bourgeois German upbringing, his philosophical under-
pinnings, his contempt for the quality and the personalities
of American politics — contributed to his attitude. And being
Mencken he said his say — loudly, bluntly, mockingly. At the
Smart Set this was felt in the countinghouse, and as a critic he
began to find himself vulnerable to *ad hominem* attacks, many of
them shockingly irrelevant and abusive, from those who had
smarted under his criticisms. At the Sunpapers the cleavage between his views and the ardently Wilsonian management of the
papers grew so broad as to be intolerable. In 1915 his "Free Lance"
column came to an end abruptly; and except for a comic opera
episode as a war correspondent for the *Sun* in Germany, which
ended with American entry into the war, his contributions to the
paper dwindled to little and then nothing. In the literary world
the counterattacks on him increased ominously with the war
fever. His *A Book of Prefaces* (1917), consisting of a series of critical studies, was viciously reviewed by, among others, Stuart Sherman. Sherman was then the leading academic critic, and his far
from academic attack amounted to this: the opinions of the man
Mencken on prose fiction are beneath contempt because he is no

patriot. Then too there was a misunderstanding with his new publisher Alfred Knopf (soon happily resolved; they were destined to have an enduring friendship). Certain other journalistic enterprises worked out unsatisfactorily, as did an interim arrangement with another publisher, his friend Philip Goodman, and the *Smart Set* found itself compelled to trim its sails.

The war years were years of misery for Mencken, carrying the brand of pro-Germanism though his loyalty as a citizen was never in real doubt. He was left with no means but his private correspondence for venting his opinions. He solved the problem — that is to say, the problem of one who must write but is constrained on all sides — by plunging into his linguistic project, *The American Language*, which had been simmering gently for a long time. The conclusion of this landmark work was being written, appropriately, as the war ended. It was a critical and popular triumph when published a year later, in 1919. The impression it made on the new college generation especially, by its style, its humor and its lightly worn scholarship, was tremendous. That same year saw also the publication of the first volume in the series of *Prejudices*, consisting of reprints from the *Smart Set*, the *Evening Sun*, and some other sources. Each new *Prejudices* volume was awaited avidly by the new Menckenites, and the series ran to six before the curtain was rung down on it in 1927. And in 1919 too Mencken resumed his formal connection with the Sunpapers, this time as editorial adviser to the publisher and as a weekly contributor to the editorial page of the *Evening Sun*. He was also available for special assignment. (His reporting of the Scopes anti-evolutionary trial in Dayton, Tennessee, yielded some of his finest descriptive writing, including his famous account of the hysterical goings-on at a back country revival meeting; yet for some reason it was never brought together in a book.)

The *Smart Set* had somehow managed to struggle through the

war years. How rough the going had been is exposed in a letter Mencken wrote to Dreiser in 1920 explaining its modest rates for contributions: "If it hadn't been for the fact that each of us has a small independent income, we'd have been down and out a dozen times. All this for your private eye. . . . I go into it simply to purge your mind of any notion that you may harbor that we are Shylocks." It now emerged basically intact, and was clearly what the new generation wanted.

In brief, the Mencken Period had begun. He offered what the times needed: a clearinghouse for the cynicism and discontents of the postwar years and a lash for their excesses wielded with alternating scorn and high good humor. The work he did in bringing out and supporting the new writers (Sinclair Lewis and Fitzgerald typically) and continuing his championing of Dreiser and Conrad and a score of others was carried on with the greatest gusto. At last he could really take literature out of the hands of the decorous and the genteel and make it something meaningful (he could not have done this had the talent not been waiting in the wings, ready for a persuasive impresario). And yet even as he reached the peak of his influence as a critic of letters he began to move out of this role and into criticism of the American mores. This was not a new role for him, of course, but it now got far more emphasis: the truth is that imaginative writing was beginning to bore him. His work for the *Evening Sun* reflected this — it ran more and more to political and social commentary. His *Prejudices* books reflected this too, the first of these being devoted almost entirely to writers and writing — what he called beautiful letters and the bozart — and the last containing hardly anything relating to current writing. The change in his interests was reflected also in the *Smart Set*, where increasingly he tacked away from literature and toward life, in spite of Nathan's persistence in the old course.

The two were in fact growing apart. In a revealing letter to literary journalist Burton Rascoe Mencken described the bases and also hinted at the limitations of their long collaboration: "Our point of contact is our complete revulsion from American sentimentality. . . . We work together amicably because we are both lonely, and need some support. . . . we come together on several essentials, e.g. our common disinclination to know authors or to belong to literary coteries, our lack of national feeling, and (perhaps most important) our similar attitudes toward money, religion, women, etc." But Nathan the complete aesthete, absorbed as always in the theater, was cold to that "show" — the excesses and absurdities of the jazz age — which so dazzled and delighted Mencken as a theme for writing.

This is really what ended that long partnership. Though Mencken had no conscious intention of neglecting the arts he wanted the emphasis placed on American life — to him, the American comedy. In addition Nathan was fairly oblivious to the shoddy trappings of the *Smart Set*, but they had begun to bother Mencken. He hankered for a "swell" review, to be Brahmin in its typographical dress if not in its contents. Knopf stood ready to back such a review, and indeed had proposed it and offered to finance it; and so, after a sufficiency of preliminary planning and wrangling, the *American Mercury* got its name, the *Smart Set* was published for the last time in December 1923, and in January 1924 the new critical review appeared in its Garamond typeface and ultra-dignified green cover. The Mencken orbit was moving toward its apogee, and the reception of the *Mercury* far exceeded the expectations of the three principals, in circulation and in acclaim. Its first issues promptly became collectors' items. The impassive Miss Golde had somehow been mislaid and was succeeded by the efficient and self-effacing Edith Lustgarten in the New York office and the equally efficient and self-effacing Rosalind Lohrfinck (known simply as Lohrfinck though Mencken professed to be dimly aware that she had a private life and even a husband) at the Baltimore end of things. Otherwise the manner of operation was not greatly different from *Smart Set* days, though quarters were moved into the Knopf office and there was a need for more of those train trips to New York.

And yet the crack in the collaboration was widening, and becoming evident even to bystanders. In a long letter to Nathan, written before the *Mercury* was many months old, Mencken, who was uneasy about the course of things, brought the matter into the open: "Its chances are not unlike those which confronted the Atlantic in the years directly after the Civil War: it has an opportunity to seize leadership of the genuinely civilized minority of Americans. . . . Our interests are too far apart. . . ." It was a plea to thresh out their differences if that were still possible, subconsciously a bid for dominance. Nathan, seeing the course of things, accepted it with good nature. After fewer than a dozen issues he abandoned his co-editorship, though he kept on as a contributor; and before the decade was over he and Mencken had parted completely — not in anger but as intellectual and emotional strangers. Mencken carried on alone, with an assistant (Charles Angoff, who proved in the end to be no friend and whose *H. L. Mencken, a Portrait from Memory*, put out in the year of Mencken's death, was a bitter and distressing performance).

The Mencken wave swept on, with the *Mercury* riding its crest; and there was hardly a page of this but showed the hand of the editor. He was at once the most ingratiating and the most exacting of editors. Contributions were responded to with unprecedented speed, and the blow of every rejection was softened by one of Mencken's inimitable notes. Rascoe once wrote: "I have yet to meet a man under thirty-five with articulate ideas who has not a sheaf of those lively, hearty notes whereby Mencken conveys a maximum of good cheer and boisterous comment within a minimum of space." Acceptance for publication brought immediate payment, and (quite unprecedented in the experience of free-lance writers) a conveyance of copyright was forthcoming immediately after publication. This act of generosity cost nothing, yet earned enormous dividends in the good will of a whole generation of young writers struggling for recognition. He was ever attentive to the legitimate interests of his contributors, yet determined always to have his way. An article with a clumsy opening, a feeble conclusion? Out with them! In with new ones from his own typewriter, but always there was advance warning along with a plea for acquiescence when he was dealing with a style-conscious writer. He was marvelous at finding the one-article man — the jailbird or the cab driver with a story to tell. He constantly tapped the well of working newspapermen, but found it shallower than one might think; of his early newspaper colleagues he once wrote: "At least half the members of the staff had literary ambitions of some sort or another, but not one of them ever got anywhere as a writer in the years following." He ransacked the campuses and the ranks of campus journalists for youngsters of promise, and gave many of them their start.

Mencken himself did but one book from the ground up, so to speak, during this period, which was the latter half of the twenties. That was not a success: his *Notes on Democracy* (1926). Even that one was mainly a rewriting job based on previously published material. It was done in such time as he could spare from his furious magazine editing, his continuing daily journalism, and responses to the calls now being made on him increasingly in his role as a unique national figure, certainly the most hated and also perhaps the most admired American of his time. These calls were of many sorts, but mainly from academe. Here is one described in a letter to Philip Goodman: "I am lecturing at Goucher College tonight: an annual affair. The audience consists of 250 virgins. I begin on the subject of national literature, but at 8.35 modulate gracefully into the Old Subject in F sharp minor. I always advise them to marry early, as, after all, the most sanitary and economically secure way of life for a Christian girl." But of course he refused dozens for every one he accepted.

The magazine itself began to show evidence of strain, of stridency. Mencken's commentaries on books continued, and at length, but there was a forced quality in much of this now, and they tended to turn into lectures on his special brand of sociology. His waning interest in literature as literature began to show in the magazine's fiction, too: having given a whole generation of new writers the stage and the audience they needed, he had slipped out of the audience, or at least was on the way to the exit. In his preoccupation with manners and morals, he actually began to miss new writing talent, worse, to misjudge it: Hemingway, for example, and Faulkner, and Thomas Wolfe. The frantic twenties were beginning to burn themselves out, and so apparently was the chief barker of this gaudiest of side shows, though by ordinary standards the magazine continued to prosper throughout the decade.

In 1929, Mencken completed the second of his trilogy treating formally of politics, religion, and morals: his *Treatise on the Gods* (1930). As Cairns remarks, he had plowed new land when he wrote *The American Language*, which was in every sense an original work, in subject as well as treatment. Religion was another matter, a preoccupation of powerful minds since the dawn of human consciousness, the most thoroughly worked field of all: small room here for originality. What he could do, and did, was to restate the materialist-rationalist position as so thoroughly developed in the nineteenth century by Huxley and others, but in contemporary terms, bringing to bear the abundant new material of psychology and the study of human institutions. He saw the religious motive as a prudent form of hedging against the terrors of the unknown, and organized religion as an elaborate tool for bamboozling and manipulating the credulous masses, a tool of government really. There was not a trace of the mystic in him, and while acknowledging the genuineness of the mystical experience he looked upon it as one of the puzzles not yet worked out by scientific means. He came by his antireligious position quite naturally, first through his grandfather Burkhardt, then through his father, then by degrees through his reading. The constant prevalence of what he felt to be a delusion had absorbed him from adolescence on. Writing of the place of religion in his family, he commented many years later to A. G. Keller, a Yale anthropologist and disciple of William Graham Sumner, "My mother went to church now and then, but her doctrinal ideas seem to have been very vague, for I never heard her mention them. I think she went simply as a sort of social gesture. My father accompanied her no more than two or three times in my recollection, and even then he went under protest. Religion was simply not a living subject in the house." Anathema to the conventionally religious, his *Treatise on the Gods* is nevertheless a storehouse of learning and curious information; and it has ample helpings of the characteristic Mencken audacity and wit. It received a far better reception than his *Notes on Democracy*, as possibly it deserved to, and it sold well. It was his last substantial success for some time, and its appearance coincided with a sharp break in what had seemed the unbreakable pattern of his private life, the tender episode of his middle-aged courtship and marriage.

In spite of the public impression to the contrary, Mencken's personal life followed a rigorous and austere routine. At the center of it was the family house in Hollins Street presided over with quiet authority by his mother Anna. The loss of her in 1925 had affected him far more than he could have anticipated, in the small ways that so quickly add up to a big way, and his correspondence is full of references to her death. To Jim Tully he wrote, for example: "You ask if I feel lonely here. My belief is that all authors are essentially lonely men. Every one of them has to do his work in a room alone, and he inevitably gets very tired of himself. My mother's death in December, 1925, left me at a loss. My sister is keeping house but the place seems empty. It is hard to reorganize one's life after 45."

It is too pat to say that he turned to Sara Haardt on the rebound. Yet without doubt his mother's death was contributory to his growing attachment to Sara and his need for the qualities she had to give. He had met her at one of those annual lectures to the Goucher College virgins. She taught there — a young lady from the deep South, a minor but fastidious novelist and short story writer with a faint aura of the anachronistic about her, reserved and physically frail. Their marriage in 1930 took all but a few of their closest friends by surprise, and was greeted with ironic delight by editorial writers from coast to coast. That the author of *In Defense of Women* and chief railer at the institution of holy matrimony should himself succumb, and be married by a parson at that! Mencken took the public ribbing in good part, and so did Sara though somewhat nervously, as they settled down to the sedate idyll which both knew, or had reason to suspect, could not last long. It was broken frequently by her illnesses, and it ended with her death five years later — a cruel blow to Mencken however much he had anticipated and prepared for it. He told Hamilton Owens shortly after her death that the doctors had given her only three years at the time of their marriage. "Actually she lived five, so that I had two more years of happiness than I had any right to expect." It had been a precious, bittersweet thing, and life in the apartment which they had established on Baltimore's handsome Mount Vernon Place, and where Sara had indulged her bent for the Victorian style, had lost its meaning. In due course he returned "completely dashed and dismayed" to the house in Hollins Street to take up life again with his brother August, his shadow from then to the end.

In the meantime other troubles of a worldly and professional kind had been piling up on him. As the times had embraced him following World War I, so now with the crash and the onset of the Great Depression they were ready to reject him. A nation dazed and hurt by the collapse of its financial and industrial structure, by farmers dispossessed and city people caught overnight with no means of subsistence, by soup lines and apple sellers and a steady shower of overextended brokers leaping out of Wall Street windows, ceased to enjoy being described as a gaudy human comedy. That kind of talk, and writing, might be tolerable and even entertaining in a going concern. To a people on the ropes, it seemed suddenly petty and irrelevant. It was a time of shocked and bitter reaction and among the victims of this was Mencken's unchanging and unchangeable devotion to individuality, self-reliance, and limited government. To his readers he ceased abruptly to be a champion of the individual and herald of freedom and became an arch-reactionary — this without changing his position one iota. His newspaper polemics seemed suddenly and oddly out of date; he lost the faith and credit of the new generation of college students (that was perhaps the worst blow save Sara's death); the circulation of the *Mercury* began to slide. One does not write easily in the face of a situation like that; and Mencken's writing showed it. The familiar refrains turned stale, the variations were no longer amusing.

One blow came after another. The decision to abandon the *Mercury* was taken in 1933 and was actually welcomed by him (it lived on for a while under another editor, then passed from hand to hand, always downward). The third of his trilogy on politics, religion, and morals, the *Treatise on Right and Wrong* (1934), got a critical mauling and had a poor sale — a far poorer sale than the same book would have had, certainly, ten years before, for it is highly readable still.

The Depression moved into what he considered the fantastic excesses of the Roosevelt New Deal. He had voted for Roosevelt while confessing privately that he thought him "a weak sister," but quickly changed his mind. So far as he was concerned, the Rooseveltian devaluation of the dollar was on a par with the coin clipping of an earlier day, which is to say a form of refined thievery; and Roosevelt's manner of doing it, which involved pulling the rug out from under his own delegation to the London Economic Conference, the behavior of a cad. Cynical as Mencken was about the courts in general and the caliber of the men who manned them, Roosevelt's scheme for packing the Supreme Court and so ensuring the color of constitutionality for whatever he might do shocked him beyond measure. The mixture of soft-voiced paternalism and political ruthlessness so finely blended in the character of Roosevelt II (as he called him) grated on his nerves like the jangle of an out-of-tune piano. "I begin to believe seriously," he wrote to the publisher B. W. Huebsch, "that the Second Coming may be at hand. Roosevelt's parodies of the Sermon on the Mount become more and more realistic. The heavens may open at any moment. Keep your suitcase packed."

As he responded in typical vein to the course of events it became clearer day by day — and to none more clearly than Mencken himself — that he was no longer being listened to. His day as reigning critic of manners and politics was over. In journalism he continued to take special assignments for the Sunpapers but he abandoned his famous *Evening Sun* Monday articles early in 1938. War was brewing again across the Atlantic, and with his

H. L. Mencken

Washingtonian belief in no foreign entanglements he was bitter-
ly against American involvement; but he saw it coming. Wish-
fully, he played down Hitler as a clown who could not long hold
the stage. To George S. Schuyler, the Negro journalist, in 1939:
"Roosevelt is hot to horn into the European mess, and his wiz-
ards believe that if he can scare the country sufficiently, it will
be possible to reelect him [for a third term] next year. I am in-
clined to agree that this is sound political dope." He dreaded the
recurrence of war fever with its intolerance, its vindictiveness,
its restraints on free expression, and at the beginning of World
War II he gave up writing regularly for the *Sun* though he remained as editorial adviser. Every superior journalist has feelers:
Mencken's told him it was time to shut up, at least so far as
public affairs were concerned.

With that durable good sense that governed him through the
downs as well as the ups of his career, he had in the meantime
turned to other things. One of the defenses he fell back on was
the labor without end that he had made for himself in American
linguistics. On returning to Hollins Street and at the bottom of
his loneliness following the death of Sara, he plunged into the
work of rewriting, enlarging, and in many ways reshaping *The
American Language* for its fourth edition. This was published in
1936. The reception of it proved that whatever may have hap-
pened to his standing as a publicist, in this other field it was
secure. Supplement I and Supplement II, massive works and complete in themselves, came along in due course (1945 and 1948).

More surprising was the way he opened an entirely new lode.
Those who knew Mencken well knew how false was the impression of his personality that his no-quarter polemical writing gave.
That was his battle dress. To be sure it was not exactly a mask,
since he loved the give and take of public controversy. But it did
conceal a much more complicated personality through which ran

27

a broad stream of sentiment and warm humanity. His love affair and marriage with Sara had exposed this briefly to an astonished public. Now, disarmed as a controversialist, he yielded to it in his writing. He turned to the recollection of his childhood in the Baltimore of another day, that childhood for which he had no regrets, in a series of sketches written for the *New Yorker* magazine. They were by turns rollicking, mordant, warmhearted, and nostalgic; and they were greeted with surprise and delight. These were brought together in his book called *Happy Days*, published in 1940. In its preface he conceded that "the record of an event is no doubt often bedizened and adulterated by my response to it," but insisted on the essential truth of the sketches as both autobiography and social history. As props to memory he had consulted his father's old accounts, miraculously intact, and other "contemporary inscriptions."

There followed in 1941 a second volume, *Newspaper Days*. This second group of autobiographical sketches, covering his first years of newspaper life in Baltimore, he described as "mainly true, but with occasional stretchers," and he commended them to the understanding sort of reader who, in Charles Lamb's phrase, felt no call to take "everything perversely in the absolute and literal sense." Absolutely and literally true they certainly were not, as for example his deathless story of "A Girl from Red Lion, P.A." They were better than that: they caught and preserved the smells and flavor and temper of an era. The success of these two volumes inspired a project for a full autobiography to be done on a scale of one book per decade; but he thought better of it: his good sense told him that the mood could not be sustained into the years of his combative maturity. He did one more book of reminiscences, *Heathen Days* (1943), which made pleasant enough reading and did well but lacked the perfect autumnal quality of its predecessors, and called quits on this enterprise.

H. L. Mencken

Mencken was coming to the end of his days as a writer. There was his book of quotations, fruit of a lifetime of clipping and marking and note-saving, and a very different thing from Bartlett's. It was published in 1940 as *A New Dictionary of Quotations*. His *Christmas Story*, a brief bit of mellow buffoonery on a sardonic theme, was published in 1946. In 1948 he returned to the Sunpapers after much urging, and reluctantly, to cover the presidential conventions of that year, including the rump convention of the Wallace Progressive party which proved to be an extravaganza made to order for his talents. The rigors of the campaign itself were no longer for him, but that fall he did contribute a few more things to the paper from home base. His last piece of newspaper writing was published on November 9 of that year, a few days after the election. It was on a subject unrelated to the election, and I will return to it a bit farther on, for it was an appropriate epitaph to a man who had spent much of his life battling for the rights of the individual.

Two weeks later he was taken by the thrombosis that ended his career with such terrible finality. One last book had occupied him toward the end of his writing years: a book of aphorisms and short statements culled from his notes. The manuscript, completed and ready for the printer, was found some years later and was published as *Minority Report: H. L. Mencken's Notebooks* following his death in 1956.

It is in character that the last four sentences of Mencken's final book (that same posthumous *Minority Report*) have to do with his style as a writer: "The imbeciles who have printed acres of comment on my books have seldom noticed the chief character of my style. It is that I write with almost scientific precision — that my meaning is never obscure. The ignorant have often complained that my vocabulary is beyond them, but that is simply because my ideas cover a wider range than theirs do. Once they have consulted the dictionary they always know exactly what I intend to say. I am as far as any writer can get from the muffled sonorities of, say, John Dewey."

It is true enough that there was never anything muffled or fuzzy (though there was plenty of sonority) about what Mencken wrote. His meaning was always transparently clear. But the passage is worth looking at closely because it illustrates how much more than that there was to the Mencken style, which is loaded with artifice. Scientific precision? On the face of it, this example is loaded with imprecisions. The word "imbeciles," for example. A great deal that had been written about Mencken's books was silly, certainly. But the men who had written about Mencken, silly though they might be, were certainly not imbeciles by any available definition of that word. Nor had they written "acres" on the subject — another flagrant inexactitude. Nor did the ignorant often complain about his vocabulary, because the ignorant did not often read him. When they did, it was not his vocabulary that bothered them. As to the elements of his vocabulary that might be complained of, resort to the dictionary was no help because they were either words of his own invention — "booboisie," "bozart" — or old words deftly provided with new meanings and bent to his special uses. His vocabulary was most definitely not beyond his readers: the complaints were from readers who understood only too well what he was saying and were responding precisely as he intended them to respond. The complaints were the flutterings of hit birds.

To write with scientific precision is to take mathematics for a model, avoiding all emotive overtones, rejecting anything that might color a plain statement of fact or interfere with the unfolding of a rational argument — to reject the art of rhetoric, in other words. But Mencken was a supreme rhetorician. Far from being scientific, his use of words was aesthetic. He used them as an artist uses color and a musician the arrangement of notes in clusters — to play upon the senses and emotions of his readers, to make them laugh, sigh, weep, go along with him, grind their teeth in fury, and to put across his point whether it was intrinsically worth making or just a piece of wayward mischief. That paragraph on style, with its deceptive bluntness, clarity, and simplicity, illustrates pretty well how much more complicated it is than he would ever admit.

For the origins of his style one can go straight back to his discovery of *Huckleberry Finn* in his ninth year, which he described as "probably the most stupendous event of my life." It was indeed. He devoured everything he could find by Mark Twain, whose manner of writing was without question the chief influence on his own. Twenty-five years later he wrote (in the *Smart Set*): "I believe that 'Huckleberry Finn' is one of the great masterpieces of the world, that it is the full equal of 'Don Quixote' and 'Robinson Crusoe' . . . I believe that it will be read by human beings of all ages, not as a solemn duty but for the honest love of it, and over and over again . . . I believe that Mark Twain had a clearer vision of life, that he came nearer to its elementals and was less deceived by its false appearances, than any other American who has ever presumed to manufacture generalizations . . . I believe that, admitting all his defects, he wrote better English, in the sense of cleaner, straighter, vivider, saner English, than either Irving or Hawthorne. . . . I believe that he was the true father of our national literature, the first genuinely American artist of the blood royal. . . . He was one of the great artists of all time. He was the full equivalent of Cervantes and Molière, Swift and Defoe. He was and is the one authentic giant of our national literature."

From Mark Twain he learned many things, never to forget

them, including these: that sentiment is nothing to be ashamed of though sentimentality is, that the way to meet human venality is to meet it head on, that compassion and a sense of humility need never be concealed, and that, in Mark Twain's words, "the secret source of Humor . . . is not joy but sorrow. There is no humor in heaven." From Mark Twain came the qualities that make Mencken the American humorist second only to Mark Twain himself. Alistair Cooke considers that Mencken has been overrated as a thinker and "underrated as a humorist with a deadly sensible eye on the behavior of the human animal." Mark Twain gave him that eye, or at least inspired him to use his own, and much of his apparatus as a writer.

There were other sources, all going back to his childhood and youth, for he was quick to discover that there are ways, and ways, of writing. Thomas Huxley fascinated him not only for what he had to teach but for his utter clarity, and he mentioned Huxley many years later as "the greatest of all masters of orderly exposition. He taught me the importance of giving to every argument a simple structure." In his view Huxley's prose "was the best produced by an Englishman in the Nineteenth Century."

At several places in his writing, Mencken points to the old New York *Sun*, "especially its editorial page," as an influence on his style, an influence both good and bad — "good because it taught me that good sense was at the bottom of all good writing, but bad because it . . . made me overestimate the value of smart phrases." There is a touch of irony in this, considering how Mencken lambasted editorial writers throughout his life: it turns out that his animus was against the third-raters, not against the competent ones.

He sucked up much from Nietzsche and Shaw and Macaulay, though he never failed to take a poke at Macaulay later on for his pretentiousness. Cooke summarizes their contributions almost too patly: "Nietzsche suggested the outlandish metaphors, Macaulay the feigned omniscience . . . Shaw taught him most." Both Shaw and Mencken, as he writes, "are superior popular educators who kick up a terrific dust on the intellectual middle plateau between the philistine and the first-rate scholar. What makes both of them more memorable than many of their betters is their style." But Mencken never had Shaw's malice and he wholly lacked "the shrill spinster note that in the end wearies all but the most dedicated of Shaw's disciples."

Shaw was, as we know, the subject of Mencken's first book. Mencken admitted that "there was a good deal of empty ornament" in that book, as in his early *Smart Set* work which came along shortly after, but that "afterward I began to tone down, and by the time I was thirty I had developed a style that was clear and alive. I can detect no diminution of its aliveness as I grow older." In this latter remark (from *Minority Report*) he is unduly modest. Of all his writing, the most flexible, subtle, and responsive to his demands was the autumn-blooming style of his autobiographical sketches.

Of stylistic characteristics peculiar to him, there were many. I mention four.

One of these was his belief that the function of criticism — coming ahead even of the discovery of the true and the beautiful — was to be interesting. He never forgot the man on the receiving end: the reader. Always before him as he wrote was the vision of a reader who might fall into a doze with a book, one of his, in his lap; or of the newspaper reader who might pause for a moment over what he had written, yawn, and move on to the next column.

Corollary to this was the care he took to be always on the offensive. He had discovered early that what the public likes is a fight. His first purpose being to catch and hold the interest of the reader, he always charged. This made for difficulties if in all

33

honesty he was compelled to bestow praise. But he had a way around that, too. "When I have to praise a writer, I always do it by attacking his enemies."

Another was his constant resort to the *reductio ad absurdum*, which as James Farrell says he often handled not only cleverly but even brilliantly. The object was to make his victim a butt of ridicule. Here he was most plainly Mark Twain's disciple, who saw laughter as the one really effective weapon of an honest man in an imperfect and on the whole inattentive world. Other weapons might, with time and diligence, make some impression on humbug, but as Mark Twain said, "only laughter can blow it to rags and atoms at a blast."

The fourth was the care with which he placed his readers, those he wanted to persuade, on his side in any argument. He wrote, as he never tired of assuring his readers, for "the nobility and gentry," for "the truly civilized minority." Anyone taking the trouble to read him could therefore consider himself complimented. By inference his readers could never possibly be identified with the bores, shams, and neanderthals whom he delighted to take apart, or share in the slightest their meanness of spirit, their stupidity, their ignorance, and their wrongheadedness. Before going into battle, Mencken always saw to it that the cheering section — his reader — was in good heart and ready to back him. He was a master at this sort of rhetorical sleight of hand.

In discussing "the Mencken philosophy," let us begin by acknowledging that Mencken was not a philosopher. Cairns calls him a positivist, and though the word is probably the right one if Mencken must be given a philosophical label, it seems curiously formal and inappropriate for one of such commonsensical cast of mind. And the tag "skeptic" used in its philosophical sense is even less appropriate. The philosophical skeptic has an open mind, he is a doubter, but he stands ready to be convinced by rational argument — if he can't break down the argument. Philosophical skepticism is apt to be the refuge of timorous but clever men since philosophical arguments can be quite easily destroyed, by the cheap and easy device of questioning the major premise if by no other, and the skeptic is thus spared on high philosophical grounds the inconvenience and vulnerability involved in taking a position on anything. Mencken was abundantly skeptical of the motives of men, especially when they purported to be lofty, and of the postures assumed by public figures. But he was no skeptic: he had a set of convictions as unshakable as Gibraltar. He knew his own mind, and as I have suggested he was not prepared to allow anyone to change it.

The point is that he was simply not interested in first causes or fine-spun theories of knowledge: metaphysics bored him; more, it enraged him, since efforts to prove the unprovable by word-defining and logic-chopping (which is the self-assigned task of metaphysicians) struck him as being the vainest of all parlor games. His view is put with utmost starkness in a famous letter to Burton Rascoe: "My notion is that all the larger human problems are insoluble, and that life is quite meaningless — a spectacle without purpose or moral. I detest all efforts to read a moral into it." But his disgust with philosophy's efforts to account for the universe and its contents, including man, did not, as I say, leave him a skeptic. He believed (and this is where the word "positivism" comes in) in the tangible, the measurable, the verifiable. He described himself once as "a materialist of the materialists," and put it another way in a letter in which he wrote of his "congenital dislike of Plato" and his preference for feet-on-the-ground Aristotle. What science could discover and verify, that he believed; and it must be admitted that during the past several hundred years science has taken a lot of territory away from philosophy.

This gave him all the base he needed for his work as what he called a "critic of ideas." It was the shooting box from which he blasted away at organized religion. It provided him with his political position, which was at once antidemocratic and passionately libertarian. It was from this point of view that he saw human beings and the whole rickety structure of human institutions.

Pushing aside formal philosophy, then, Mencken started with the proposition (certainly verifiable) that the human organism despite its manifold wonders is a badly botched job. ("God nodded," he once exploded in the midst of the hay fever season, "when he designed my nose.") From that he moved on to the proposition (also verifiable) that all men are not created equal. Equal they may be, or should be, before the law, and equally entitled to opportunity; but demonstrably they are not equal in their native physical and intellectual endowment. The natural incompetence and gullibility of the masses he held to be a matter of simple fact, confirmed every day and everywhere, and the existence in much smaller numbers of superior men a matter equally beyond dispute.

And from this, though he had nothing better to offer ("I am interested in pathology, not therapeutics"), came his criticism of democratic theory and practice. The mass of men, buffeted by forces beyond their strength and understanding, do not yearn for freedom but for security. They turn automatically to the man who promises this. They are the natural prey of demagogues always ready to exploit them for their own purposes, and no system is better adapted to demagoguery than popular democracy. Democracy always and inevitably tends toward mobocracy.

But nothing could be more mistaken than to assume from this that Mencken would have preferred any totalitarian form. He detested Hitler and Mussolini and every other kind of demagogue either hard or soft. His concern was simply that under popular democracy, in which decisions are so often motivated by appeals to envy and promises of something for nothing, the victims are the superior man, the creative man, the self-respecting man — "the only sort of man who is really worth hell room, to wit, the man who practises some useful trade in a competent manner, makes a decent living at it, pays his own way, and asks only to be let alone. He is now a pariah in all so-called civilized countries." Mencken's bill of particulars against democracy boiled down to his simple belief that democracy, given its head, dislikes and hamstrings the producer and the creator.

Though he never put it that way, Mencken was in fact a strict constitutionalist. Given a constitution beyond the reach of easy amendment, that is to say a set of rules that did really restrain the mob and its masters, that put limitations on government and made them stick, kept speech free, and provided equal justice, the superior man probably had as good a chance as under any other conceivable system. But where is the constitution that is invulnerable to the mob when it has really been inflamed? His own experience as a critic of national policy in two world wars left him with small faith in the protections of the United States Constitution or any other. It is interesting that Mencken's political ideas are taken far more seriously in Europe today, among those familiar with them, than they are in his native land. Europeans have more, and more bitter, memories of curdled democracy than Americans do.

A study of Mencken's political ideas necessarily begins with his *Notes on Democracy*. But this is marred by a certain stridency and an overindulgence in bathos and paradox. His ideas somehow come out better in his topical writings on political issues and personalities. Most of the best of these things are brought together in *On Politics: A Carnival of Buncombe*, edited by Malcolm Moos, and in *Prejudices: A Selection*, edited by James T. Farrell.

They amplify the comments on his philosophy which are offered above.

Mencken's ingrained habit of calling things and people by their right names, and his clear-eyed refusal to confuse what is what with what ought or ought not to be, led people into false inferences about his likes and prejudices. What he disliked above all was pretense. "As I say, all my work hangs together. Whether it appears to be burlesque, or serious criticism, or mere casual controversy, it is always directed against one thing: unwarranted pretension." Thus he referred to Jews as matter-of-factly as he referred to Methodists, jested about Jewish traits that to him seemed comic, criticized specifically Jewish activities that he thought harmful. This to L. M. Birkhead, a Unitarian pastor, is illustrative: "I believe there is another difficulty in the anti-Semitic question. After all, a man who believes sincerely that the Jews are a menace to the United States ought to be allowed to say so. The fact that he is wrong has got nothing whatsoever to do with it. The right to free speech involves inevitably the right to talk nonsense. I am much disturbed by the effort of the New York Jews to put down criticism. It seems to me that they are only driving it underground, and so making it more violent." This was Mencken talking free speech, not anti-Semitism. He cared nothing for racial or social stigmata and looked past them to the man. A small expression of this is that one of the two well-known paintings of him was done by a Jew, the other by a Negro.

And so it was with his jocosities about "the colored brethren" which reflected the mores of his time and the culture of the Negro community in Baltimore then and throughout the country generally. He didn't pretend not to notice differences. And yet the very last thing he wrote, the article in the *Evening Sun* of November 9, 1948, which I have already mentioned, was an angry protest against the conviction of a mixed group of seven who had challenged Baltimore's segregation ordinances by staging what he called "an interracial tennis combat" on the courts of a public park. "Is such a prohibition . . ." he asked, "supported by anything to be found in common sense and common decency? . . . My answer . . . is a loud and unequivocal No. A free citizen in a free state, it seems to me, has an inalienable right to play with whomsoever he will, so long as he does not disturb the general peace. If any other citizen, offended by the spectacle, makes a pother, then that other citizen, and not the man exercising his inalienable right, should be put down by the police."

No sturdier defender of civil liberties has ever lived, and it was in character that he should have ended his writing, as a newspaperman grinding the grist of the news, with a simple statement supporting them.

The public Mencken, as I hope I have made clear, was different in many ways from the private Mencken. To the public generally, and especially after the press took to quoting him on anything and everything in the late twenties and early thirties, he was a roistering fellow who had an acid tongue and a club in his hand and was given to every sort of excess. He went along with this cheerfully, and even encouraged it. Why not? It gave him an instant audience, one running into the millions, for anything he might want to say. Others might coat their pills with sugar: he used a tart and astringent coating and found the public equally ready to swallow it. His role as the arch enemy of Prohibition gave him a supplementary reputation as a fearful boozer.

His manner in company somewhat fortified that larger, vaguer reputation. In a gathering that was large and mixed he could be subdued and even ill at ease, but among men whom he found congenial he was a marvelous companion — exuberant, boisterous, often ribald. I recall his daily visits to the Sunpapers back in the days when I was a green young editorial writer. His loud greeting was at once gay and gruff. He would disappear into one sanctum or another, that of the editor or the publisher, and from behind the door would issue muffled roars of laughter. It wasn't the response to a monologue, quite. He dominated, but he knew the difference between conversation and a one-man show. He enjoyed practical jokes, and often gave them a sharp edge — as for instance that fake institution known as "The Loyal Legion of American Mothers," which was "dedicated to avoiding foreign entanglements and keeping American womanhood pure." Much mischief was done under that and other equally grotesque letterheads.

But all this exuberance, and much of his enormous correspondence, were the compensations of a lonely man, a loneliness implicit in his work. In his *Minority Report* there is this: "I know a great many more people than most men, and in wider and more diverse circles, yet my life is essentially one of isolation, and so is that of every other man. We not only have to die alone; we also, save for a few close associates, have to live alone." And the bleakness of his view of the nature of things only fortified the loneliness and pessimism. "The natural state of a reflective man," he wrote in another context, "is one of pessimism."

His private life, save for some exceptions to be noted, was orderly and austere. After breakfast his day began with an hour or two of dictation to Lohrfinck, his secretary. When she had gone, he worked until noon on his notes and files and some writing; following luncheon he put on his public manner for his daily visit to the Sunpapers, with arrival punctually at two o'clock. By mid-afternoon he was in Hollins Street again to work on his papers until about five. Then a book, or the better part of one, perhaps a brief nap, the return of Lohrfinck with a load of letters to sign and seal, and a short walk to the mailbox before his supper (his concession to exercise); after supper, which was finished before eight, came his main bout of writing for the day in his third-floor quarters, which normally stretched on to about ten o'clock; then downstairs to unwind, usually with his brother August, or out to Schellhase's, a *gemütlich* little restaurant, for a couple of glasses of beer with an old friend or two; and then home to bed not long after eleven o'clock, to read until he fell asleep.

There was not much room in such a routine for roistering. His weekly letdown came on Saturday nights with an odd assortment of cronies who made up the Saturday Night Club. They met in the early days above Al Hildebrand's fiddle shop, to grind out music together, Mencken at the piano with a heavy hand. Later they had a second-floor room at Schellhase's; and after the music there was beer and merriment. Music was Mencken's avocation, his companion and pleasure throughout his life: "I'd rather have written any symphony of Brahms' than any play of Ibsen's. I'd rather have written the first movement of Beethoven's Eroica than the Song of Solomon . . . In music a man can let himself go. In words he always remains a bit stiff and unconvincing." His musician friend Louis Cheslock, possibly a prejudiced witness, always insisted that "in the same sense that Beethoven was aware of the language of sound, Mencken was aware of the sound of language."

His other recreation, growing out of his hypochondriacal temperament, was hospital visiting. Ill health, to him, was the great human curse and calamity; and that sympathy for human suffering, that compassion for the lot of man in general which he kept so well concealed from his larger public, got its release out of visits to the sick. He was a familiar figure in the halls of Johns Hopkins Hospital and of all the other local pesthouses, as he liked to call them.

He traveled occasionally, but the preparations had a way of turning into crises, and the chief effect of such holidays was to make him long for the familiar ambiance of Baltimore and the routine of home.

As for his reputation as a formidable boozer, it was without basis. As a youngster on the police beat (he tells in one of his sketches) he learned the lesson from a tough old fire department surgeon whom he came to know and admire that alcohol is not a stimulant but a depressant: "His words . . . continue to lurk in my mind, to this day. In consequence . . . I employ it of an evening, not to hooch up my faculties but to let them down after work. Not in years have I ever written anything with so much as a glass of beer in my system. My compositions, I gather, sometimes seem boozy to the nobility and gentry, but they are actually done as soberly as those of William Dean Howells." He was always from adolescence onward a "cagey" drinker — the first to raise his glass, but the last to empty it. He had no real taste for spirits and was forever finding excuses to avoid them.

A man always strict with himself, a disciplined man who severely rationed his pleasures, this was Mencken. To James Farrell he once said this: "Farrell, if you want to develop further as a writer, there are three things to stay away from. Booze . . . women . . . and politics." If he said that to one young writer, he said it to a hundred; and he followed his own prescription.

Mencken's output was prodigious. The Adler bibliography runs to 349 pages, and even this formidable listing excludes his letters. Guy Forgue, in the preface to his admirably edited selection of these letters, estimates that those deposited in public libraries and private collections must run to around 15,000. It is an estimate very much on the low side. Some years ago I discussed the output of Mencken letters with his brother August and mentioned 50,000 as a not unlikely number. August had lately made an estimate — not by trying to count, but by weight — of the number of letters addressed to Mencken in connection with a single work, *The American Language*, and came up with the figure of 65,000. Although this was an estimate of letters received, it also meant 65,000 replies, because Mencken's red-letter rule was to answer all letters and on the day of their receipt. What the total output of all kinds must have been, long ones and short ones, others amounting to essays, is anyone's guess. And the odd thing is that every one of these, no matter how perfunctory, was relieved by a phrase, a suggestion, a sharp comment, a touch of grotesquerie that made it hard to throw away. As for his longer letters, when he rolled up his sleeves and really went to work, some are Mencken at his best, as critic of life and letters and as self-revelation. Forgue's collection, of letters to writers mostly, is in fact one of Mencken's most absorbing books.

Mencken has been spared, fortunately, the deadly Collected Edition which abandons discrimination for comprehensiveness and which serves as a tombstone for so many writers whose work, in part, might otherwise live. As a newspaperman he wrote most of the time for the moment; but as Alistair Cooke quite properly insists there is a great deal of life, maybe immortality, in a fair bit of that stuff. The thing to do is to let time winnow it. The process is well begun in the several selections of his *Prejudices* and newspaper political pieces by Cooke, Farrell, and Moos and in Cheslock's gathering of his pieces on music. A much fuller anthology by Huntington Cairns, called *H. L. Mencken: The American Scene*, ranges all across his work and with sound judgment. Certain storehouses of Mencken material, notably the Mencken room in the Enoch Pratt Free Library of Baltimore and the New York Public Library collection, offer ripe pickings for the future.

Of his formal treatises — his *Notes on Democracy, A Treatise on the Gods*, and *A Treatise on Right and Wrong* — what is likely to be the verdict? He obviously put great store by them as a distillation of his views on the three abiding human preoccupations, with politics (or the art of living together without too much trouble) and with religion and morals (together, the art of living with oneself). But neither as a corpus nor individually can they really be called successful. The first, as suggested already, is badly organized, undisciplined, and shrill despite many a penetrating and cathartic paragraph. It overstates. It leaves the reader, shall we say, not quite persuaded. Its leading ideas are set forth better anyway in his posthumous *Minority Report*, a book which will continue to appeal to readers with a taste for the aphoristic form, and in his journalism, where they are illuminated by concrete issues and people. As for *A Treatise on the Gods* and *A Treatise on Right and Wrong*, both smell too strongly of the lamp, which is to say that they seem somehow concocted. The reading that went into them was extraordinarily wide. They contain much curious information. But Mencken's concern to make them *interesting*, to "fetch" the reader, seems inappropriate to what at bottom were intended as sober and deadly serious treatises. One is left with the conviction, again, that his leading ideas were better put by the thinkers from whom he absorbed them, that he added relatively little of his own beyond the form of the statement, that in any case they are far better stated in his topical writing and that he is not at his best in the sustained development of ideas. Mencken was simply not a systematist.

The one exception to that generalization is his great *The American Language*. And it is not hard to see why. Here Mencken the stylist, Mencken the word-juggler, is at work investigating the raw materials of his own great talent and constant preoccupation. He is studying his native tongue, his own means of communication — its origin, its evolution, the springs that feed it, its marvelous suppleness and fluidity. The theme needed systematic exploration, for it had never been given this before; and it took a man sensitive to every nuance of speech and writing to do it. Mencken was that man; and his fascination as well as his supreme capacity for the task shows through as it does nowhere in the three efforts at systematization mentioned above.

Yet *The American Language* comes up against another fate. It deals with a living and changing thing. Even in the course of its four editions (the first in 1919 and the fourth in 1936) the growth and change of the language required many modifications, including modifications of the central thesis. The American language having grown away from British English, the two had begun to coalesce again through a reverse process: the modification of British English along American lines by extensive borrowings. McDavid's one-volume abridgment (1963) required much more than abridgment: it required extensive updating. The original *American Language* will live as a period piece, a monumental work of scholarship fixing the language as of its time, like a still shot from a film, and full of wit and wisdom. But the title shows signs of developing a life of its own, like Bartlett, Webster, Roget, and even Fanny Farmer.

If we leave out this singular case, the surest candidates for immortality seem to be his *Happy Days* and *Newspaper Days*, redolent of a life that is gone yet no more to be forgotten than the Wild West, and done in a style ripened and purged of excess, a style that as Cooke says is "flexible, fancy-free, ribald, and always beautifully lucid; a native product unlike any other style in the language." Those books and the best of his "transient" work: they are the essential Mencken. They are what he gave to our literature which time is least likely to tarnish or erode.

↙ Selected Bibliography

Principal Works of H. L. Mencken

George Bernard Shaw: His Plays. Boston: Luce, 1905.

The Philosophy of Friedrich Nietzsche. Boston: Luce, 1908.

A Book of Burlesques. New York: Lane, 1916. Revised edition, New York: Knopf, 1920.

A Book of Prefaces. New York: Knopf, 1917.

In Defense of Women. New York: Goodman, 1918. Revised edition with new Introduction, New York: Knopf, 1922.

The American Language. New York: Knopf, 1919. Second edition revised and enlarged, 1921. Third edition, revised and enlarged, 1923. Fourth edition, enlarged and rewritten, 1936.

Prejudices: First Series. New York: Knopf, 1919.

Prejudices: Second Series. New York: Knopf, 1920.

Prejudices: Third Series. New York: Knopf, 1922.

Prejudices: Fourth Series. New York: Knopf, 1924.

Notes on Democracy. New York: Knopf, 1926.

Prejudices: Fifth Series. New York: Knopf, 1926.

Prejudices: Sixth Series. New York: Knopf, 1927.

Treatise on the Gods. New York, London: Knopf, 1930.

Making a President: A Footnote to the Saga of Democracy. New York: Knopf, 1932.

Treatise on Right and Wrong. New York: Knopf, 1934.

Happy Days, 1880–1892. New York: Knopf, 1940.

Newspaper Days, 1899–1906. New York: Knopf, 1941.

Heathen Days, 1890–1936. New York: Knopf, 1943.

The American Language: Supplement One. New York: Knopf, 1945.

Christmas Story. Illustrated by Bill Crawford. New York: Knopf, 1946.

The American Language: Supplement Two. New York: Knopf, 1948.

Minority Report: H. L. Mencken's Notebooks. New York: Knopf, 1956.

Selected Editions of Works and Letters

The American Language, abridged with annotations and new material by Raven I. McDavid, Jr. New York: Knopf, 1963.

A Bathtub Hoax and Other Blasts and Bravos from the Chicago Tribune, edited by Robert McHugh. New York: Knopf, 1958.

Selected Bibliography

H. L. Mencken: The American Scene, a Reader, selected and edited with an Introduction and Commentary by Huntington Cairns. New York: Knopf, 1965.

H. L. Mencken on Music, selected by Louis Cheslock. New York: Knopf, 1961.

Letters of H. L. Mencken, selected and annotated by Guy J. Forgue with a Personal Note by Hamilton Owens. New York: Knopf, 1961.

A Mencken Chrestomathy, edited and annotated by the author. New York: Knopf, 1949.

Current American Reprints

On Politics: A Carnival of Buncombe, edited by Malcolm Moos. New York: Vintage (Knopf). $1.45.

Prejudices: A Selection, edited by James T. Farrell. New York: Vintage. $1.45.

Treatise on the Gods. New York: Vintage. $1.95.

The Vintage Mencken, gathered by Alistair Cooke. New York: Vintage. $1.45.

Bibliographies

Adler, Betty, with the assistance of Jane Wilhelm. *H. L. M.: The Mencken Bibliography*. Baltimore: Johns Hopkins Press for Enoch Pratt Free Library, 1961. (Lists, so far as can be ascertained, Mencken's shorter works, newspaper and magazine contributions, and miscellaneous writings, as well as his books; also lists critical studies of Mencken and his work, including many brief studies, published and unpublished.)

Frey, Carroll. *A Bibliography of the Writings of H. L. Mencken*, with a Foreword by H. L. Mencken. Philadelphia: Centaur Bookshop, 1924.

Porter, Bernard H. *H. L. Mencken, a Bibliography*. Pasadena: Geddes Press, 1957.

Swan, Bradford F. *Making a Mencken Collection*. New Haven: Yale University Gazette, 1950.

Critical and Biographical Studies

Angoff, Charles. *H. L. Mencken, a Portrait from Memory*. New York: Yoseloff, 1956.

Boyd, Ernest Augustus. *H. L. Mencken*. New York: McBride, 1925.

DeCasseres, Benjamin. *Mencken and Shaw, the Anatomy of America's Voltaire and England's Other John Bull*. New York: Silas Newton, 1930.

Goldberg, Isaac. *H. L. Mencken*. Girard, Kansas: Haldeman-Julius, 1920.

_____. *The Man Mencken, a Biographical and Critical Survey*. New York: Simon, 1925.

H. L. Mencken, a reprint of three articles: "Fanfare" by Burton Rascoe; "The

American Critic" by Vincent O'Sullivan; "Bibliography" by F. C. Henderson. New York: Knopf, 1920.

Kemler, Edgar. *The Irreverent Mr. Mencken.* Boston: Little, Brown, 1950.

Manchester, William. *Disturber of the Peace: The Life of H. L. Mencken,* with an Introduction by Gerald W. Johnson. New York: Harper, 1951.

Wagner, Philip M. "Mencken Remembered," *American Scholar,* 32:256–74 (Spring 1963).